The Empty Horizon

Paul Terence Carney

LIVE CANON

First Published in 2017
By Live Canon Ltd
www.livecanon.co.uk

All rights reserved

© Paul Terence Carney 2017

978-1909703322

The right of Paul Terence Carney to be identified as author of this work has been asserted by him in accordance with Section 77 of the Copyright, Design and Patents Act 1988.

All rights reserved. No part of this publication may be reproduced, stored in or introduced into a retrieval system, or transmitted, in any form, or by any means (electronic, mechanical, photocopying, recording or otherwise) without the prior written permission of the publisher. Any person who does any unauthorized act in relation to this publication may be liable to criminal prosecution and civil claims for damages.

A CIP catalogue record for this book is available from the British Library.

This book is sold subject to the condition that it shall not, by way of trade or otherwise, be lent, re-sold, hired out, or otherwise circulated without the publisher's prior consent in any form of binding or cover other than that in which it is published and without a similar condition including this condition being imposed on the subsequent purchaser.

Cover Image: John William Waterhouse's 'Miranda' (1875)

... let it suffice that she lived there by the sea, and kings ruled, and demons ruled, and kings came again, and still she abided there...

Lord Dunsany

Acknowledgments: 'When We Come Out of the West' was first published in *Acumen* (Issue 78, January 2014). 'A Room in the City' won 3rd prize in the Poetry London competition, 2015, and was published in *Poetry London* (Issue 82, Autumn 2015) and in Live Canon's *New Poems for Christmas* anthology (2015). 'Monster Child' was longlisted for the National Poetry Competition 2013. 'Brian of the North' won the Borough Prize in the Live Canon International Poetry Competition, 2014, and appears in the *2014 Live Canon Anthology*. 'Half-remembered Books' was longlisted for the National Poetry Competition twice; in 2014 and 2015. 'In a Dawlish Telephone Box' was shortlisted in the Live Canon International Competition, 2015, and appears in the *2015 Live Canon Anthology*. Many of the poems in this collection were part of the poet's Master's portfolio at Goldsmith's College, University of London, which received the Pat Kavanagh Award, given by United Agents in conjunction with Goldsmith's.

Thanks are due to Helen Eastman and all at Live Canon, to Glyn Maxwell. Whilst working on the poems that form this collection, I have received invaluable advice and support from tutors, fellow students, workshop colleagues and others; in particular, Maura Dooley, Stephen Knight, Eva Salzman, Francis Spufford, John Wilks, Kate Owens, Derek Adams, Bernadette Reed, Elly Parsons, William Wyld, Sarah Bakewell, Charlotte Lindsay, Esther Boulton, Melita Kolin, Karen Storey, Bex Couper, Reuben Roy Smith, Derek Adams, Mary Lucille Hindmarch, Martin Hollins, Orlanda Marsden who has gone to great lengths to help me gain experience appearing and reading in public (preparatory to my release into the wild), and, most especially, Barbara Marsh, who has taught, guided, inspired and somehow put up with me for the past seven years and who, more than anyone, has earned what Seamus Heaney called "that special kind of gratitude we reserve for those who lead us toward confidence in ourselves".

Contents

Introduction	i
Half-remembered Books	1
In the Others' House	3
Roisin and the Stars	5
Brian of the North	6
A Synopsis	7
A Crow, Translated into the Irish	8
Bestiary for a Painted Earth	9
An Hour from the River	11
Sainsbury's Trout	13
In a Dawlish Telephone Box	14
Pigeons After Dark	16
Roisin's Dream of Escape	17
Tinea trinotella	19
When We Come Out of the West	20
Black Swans at Sunrise	22
The Art of Self-portraiture	23
If We Should Ever Meet	25
Mice Will Sing on the Sea	28
Monster Child (Roisin Leaves a Note)	31
These Notes Were for a Sequel, Never Finished	33
A Room in the City	35
Notes	37

Introduction

This sequence of poems concerns the plight of Roisin, a writer and illustrator of children's books who is losing her sight due to the genetic condition *Retinitis Pigmentosa*. As if encroaching blindness were not bad enough, she is effectively stranded in a condemned Victorian house on the edge of the small South Devon town of Dawlish, in a crumbling room beneath a pigeon-haunted attic, overlooking the railway and the sea.

She is there because, being an artist, she has no money, and has found herself living in the spare room of a family of West Country hippies, whom she has come to think of only as *the Others*. The Others were initially her friends, and the arrangement began with her doing some babysitting and other household chores in lieu of rent. But over time, these friends have become increasingly needy and dependent, and Roisin has effectively become their household slave. She is held there partly by her concern for the youngest of the children she looks after, but primarily by having nowhere else to go, and by being literally unable to find the escape route. (A curious thing about being visually impaired in Dawlish is that while it seems you cannot get away from the noise of that bloody railway, it can be remarkably difficult to locate the station.)

In what little free time she has, Roisin is trying to persevere with work on a book about a child in medieval Ireland in the time of Saint Patrick, who believes he has been instructed by God to travel to Britain, find the snakes wrongly banished by the Saint, and bring them home.

Roisin is so isolated that her only regular human contact outside the House of Others is her editor, Brian, whom she has never met in person, but whose voice on the telephone has a lovely, deep Northern accent. On this basis, she has constructed a mental image of him as a literate-but-ruggedly-windswept Man of the Outdoors – a kind of Ted Hughes figure – who, when not at his desk in the publisher's office, goes striding over the moors, communing with Nature and so forth, and who just might, if she is worthy, even come stomping all the way to Dawlish, to find her and make everything alright.

Half-remembered Books

The crunch in the bones of my neck is like boots
marching on gravel. My hair feels so coarse,
and it sounds on the pillow like withered grass roots
being torn up and champed by a ravenous horse.
My heart beats as loud as the waves at the wall,
and fast as the night trains that ferry the souls
of the damned into Dawlish. I feel myself fall,
and I clutch at my blanket. Down the black holes
of my eyes dance bananas of migrainous light,
and I am a long way from sleep. Now the dark
crowds with years-ago things; like the sight
of a picture-book blowing away in the park –
every lost snowflake picked out in white paint
by someone who's probably dead. All the books
I don't have anymore, like the one with the saint
who was fed as an infant by seagulls. Or rooks.
And the one where a cat played a small ukulele
and sang the most libellous songs; and another –
with full-colour pictures – of Bad Scottish Hayley
who lived on a farm, where her savage stepmother
was eaten by pigs. I glimpse fragments, as though
through the cracks in my coffin, and just out of reach
there is daylight. I sit up and struggle to slow
down my breathing. The ocean is grinding the beach
and the walls press so close. I shall never know now
what befell my first hero, the slug – or the snail –

who got lost in the forest of rhubarb; or how
the Chinese built a town on the back of that whale.
The mongrel who dug up weird bones on the moon
and the gentle brunette with her translucent-wings
are faded, and I am locked out from a room
where binoculars, beach balls and buckets and things
were my own, and I hardly had headaches at all;
where I climbed into bed every night, just before
eight, and the Seekers would sing through the wall,
while the light on the landing shone under the door.

In the Others' House

I've brought fresh coffee to your mother's bedside.
The toast was burnt, so I shall have to fetch some more.
I am to tell them, she won't be getting up today.
And when the doctor calls with the Valium suppository,
she will need me back upstairs, to hold her hand.
I've filled her cat with cubes of rabbit-corpse
in jelly, told lies to her social worker, holding the phone
with one shoulder as I poured the tea.
Your father sits cross-legged on the couch,
strums a dirge on an out-of-tune guitar, and sings

about the pain of being born, while all their friends
skin up, sniggering, around the kitchen table,
and leer at a Mona Lisa with a spliff, smirking high
above the fireplace. Your big brother hoots in the hall –
he's found a fresh dead pigeon for his ventriloquist routine.
The splintered legs and stuffing of the nursing chair
are burning in the dustbin in the yard. I'll douse the ashes
with grey water, when I've washed the breakfast things.
I've opened the windows on the top floor,
so all the new flies of the morning are gone
to find their fate on the warm September breeze.
And now, I've brought clean sheets

for you. The heavy milk in my pocket is warm as blood
against my hip. And if, as I bend to lift you up,
the room should spin around us, I will hold you

tight to my ribs, and croak an Irish lullaby,
until it slows. Then I shall nest you in white linen,
safe among the bars of your wooden cage.
The screams and breaking glass along the landing
will be no louder than the passing trains of Hell,
rattling the windows. And I will slump me down to sleep
against the wall. They shouldn't miss me for a while, and we

might drowse for long enough to share that dream
again, where I can carry you in the bend of one arm,
in the deep folds of my coat; run down all the stairs,
and never miss my footing; where I can leap
over the dog in the doorway, and go with you
in impossible moonlight, by river boat,
by horse, by stolen bicycle, all the way back
to London, where we lose ourselves
among the morning crowds.

Roisin and the Stars

Winter crane-flies always used to gather
over our first garden, where I made
my own new fossils from fallen leaves and clay.
The knobbled forms in the greenhouse windows looked
like tadpoles in amber; so I dreamed for them,
stories of how they came to be entombed.
I had a book, with joined-up stars all spread

on thick, blue pages; showing how the night
was crowded with princesses and Greek heroes
and swans. I see myself, in white pyjamas,
flapping downstairs, and out, on prickly grass –
my nostrils tugging in wood-smoke and a tang
of autumn's last beheaded marigolds –
fumbling along the conifer hedge, then standing,

peering straight up, through toy binoculars,
into a black, empty sky.

Brian of the North

In this moment, until
some secretary comes hovering
about his ear, with her mosquito-whine,
mine is the last voice he has heard – my words
are *in* him. The office chair that cannot hold him fast
creaks like a fence-post in the autumn wind as he leans back,
swinging his head to the sky in the window, thinking
of *me*.
      My hand shakes as I set the phone down,
like after-tremors of his laugh. I am unzipping, sloughing,
crawling out of jumper, jeans and sweat, and everything
(except my glasses). Naked, I hear the planes, and the sea
is louder than before, upon the rocks. Draughts clutch at me
as I present myself and ask the mirror in the wardrobe,
would I do?
      These pinhole pieces add up to a blur –
a figure in cloud. I comb my hair into submission
and wrench these scrawny shoulders back until it hurts,
striking a Vargas girl pose. I hold my breath and strive to seem
his *Barleybright*.
      This sight of me would make him laugh again,
and swathe me in that laughter like a warm, rough blanket
over all my skin. His hands would reach about me –
those bark-and-leather hands that lift to greet the dawn
between the hills; that rub the rumps of trembling horses,
break the bars of Larsen traps and raise lost magpies to the sky.
Those hands upon my shoulder-blades would pull me close –
pollen, soil and oak tree sap, wool at my cheek, and I
would stretch my arms and hook my fingers
in his hair; safe from engine-noise
and falling slates; from rain
and bitter sunlight.

A Synopsis

may come. In time. But now, I only have
these few impressions for you – vague
as though I see them through my misted breath
on glass: the Adze-head, robed and mitred, shouting down
the shepherds from the highest hilltop, brandishing
his crooked stick and tearing fistfuls of young clover

out of the soil; a few lines of the drinking song
his giant henchmen sing as they go, digging
for gold among the grave mounds; children, scrubbed
and mouth-soaped, sitting in straight ranks, inside

a new-built wooden parish hall, to learn
their hymns – on one bench, there's a vacant place;
a whispered prayer for solid ground with every fugitive
footstep in utter darkness, on a night so still that you can hear

the sinners' cattle, calling from the caverns far below the fields
where no grass grows; the sussuration of a chafer beetle's flight
in clearings, where the oak trees used to stand, where deer
and Druids dreamed in shadows; quiet whispers of a question, stirring
the weeds about the midden, endlessly; *What has became of all
my snakes? Where are they gone?*

A Crow, Translated into the Irish

His skull makes Mesozoic shadows on
my windowsill. So long ago I found him,
fallen amid bright grass, in sunlight. Then,
I sat for days, cross-legged in the garden,
ignored the sky, and measured all of him;
the curvature of his bill; the length of each
primary feather; copying the arc
of every claw, as out of numbers came
his form, in pencilled lines and scribbled notes
that no one ever saw. And he was paper
filed in a drawer, and a box of little bones –
relics of one brief summer. Once, I used
a memory of the softness of his plumage
to make a simile for someone's hair
brushing my face. And that, for years, was all

there was of him. For this, his resurrection,
he'll wear a new grey mantle; he will perch
upon the thin left shoulder of a child
to balance out the angel on the right.
He will be devious, of course. But funny.
The lullabies he sometimes sings will be
jumbled, tuneless – and sweet. He'll constantly
question the dictates of my imagined Heaven,
and he will carry in his feathers all
the scents of grass and soil, and trees, far out
across the dismal sea where he must go.

Bestiary for a Painted Earth

I
What have I seen of kingfishers,
hares and hawks? Who can say
they are real? I leave them out of it.

II
I claim the heron for a totem;
I watched him rise from the island
when I could see across the lake
and I was smaller than the span of his wings.

III
A few strokes of the brush
for the weary fox of Peckham,
rat-tailed with mange, who played
his own sad theme on dustbin lids
under my window; now he runs,
a russet streak, through all
the blue-green dreams of mallards.

IV
In these summer months,
even the wicked shall walk
in a babble of unseen finches.

V
Cats will drop in the night
like bags of sugar and soot
out of the trees
upon the sleeping traveller.

VI
Death's-head moths are carried
on the hot wind from the south
and fly among the beehives
at twilight, laughing
like the ghosts of mice.

An Hour from the River

I climb up on my desk to push the window
open, to breathe, to reach and catch the rain,
then touch my tongue on trails of light in water
over my skin. These strings of cold rain bind me
still, with the clouds, the wind, the moan of gulls
like babies on the roof; with anything

out there. When I was hoovering downstairs,
I found the Others' *A to Z of Devon*.
And there were all those river-names I've known
since I was eight, reading by battery-torchlight
under the starchy bedsheets – places far

from antiseptic smells, far from the mumble
of night-shift nurses – names in borrowed dreams
I never stopped returning to – of stars,
of stone-and-water songs, and tangled roots,
the gleams of dreaming fish, an old man's laughter
in autumn, by a waterfall. And all
the things I've never seen are just an hour

away. The paragraphs I've always known
are in your voice now. If I'm good enough,
and if you ever come, perhaps you might
take me – just once – out on the north-west road
and let me be outside, in air and earth
and flowing water. If my head is filled

with sunlight, then the pain will only be
one piece of everything. And here is how
I think of it: we go upon our bellies
and elbows through the hairy tops of grass
and oolypuggers to the edge, and there,
I lean so close, my hair is drenched, and stare
through flashing ripples like my migraine-lights –
and wait, and keep on waiting on the moment
of clarity, when all the pollywiggles
and caddis-nymphs and shrimps and every grain
of gravel comes in focus, while you stroke
my back, and read to me, about the mouse,
the mending of the kelt, the leaning alders…

And after, when I cannot climb the oak,
you climb it for me, as I feel my flesh
against the cragscape of its bark. You speak
from your all-seeing height, about the rooks
above the fields, the hedges and the haystacks,
the ream of something swimming fast below
the middle arch of Humpy Bridge. And last,
you even see and tell about the mayflies

rising. I close my eyes to picture them
the way I've dreamed them – coloured lithographs
in library books, made tiny, multiplied
a hundred thousand times, all swirling up
and up into the burning blue and white.

Sainsbury's Trout

I thought his fins would feel
like cellophane; instead, they're thick, like rubber.
I note their measurements, and then I sketch
the convex washer-ring of his eye. I work

the gadget of his mouth – see how the maxillaries
swing forward – and I press my thumb upon
his fretsaw teeth. I stroke the minute beadwork
of scales, daubed in black spots. He is so fresh –
so new to death – perhaps he languished in a tank

just yesterday, and gulped recycled water, staring up
at wavering stripes of light. He's been
unzipped; swim-bladder, heart and guts,
all gone. His flanks are like
my emptied pencil case.

In a Dawlish Telephone Box

If you can take a message; would you tell him
he cannot reach me on the usual number
these days, since the phone went out the window
(someone was aiming for someone else's head).
Be sure to say that I walked into town;
I've started taking his advice; this morning
I wandered nearly twice as far as last time
and, like he said, imagined him beside me,

keeping me safe – and I was nearly killed
by a speeding ice-cream van. So, you might mention –
he rather fucked up there. The seagulls snigger
from the rooftops. If he were on the line
I'd hold the phone out so that he could catch
the blast of country music from the Lawns –
it's Open Air Line-dancing Day; onstage

the spangled bodies lurch and hop, like corpses
strung on elastic. Tomorrow – falconry.
A brass band too. The days are so long here.
And tell him the Red Arrows were up – again –
scrawling bloody clawmarks across the clouds.
I don't bother looking up. But tell him,

oh tell him he should see the pigeons coming
home to their holes in the roof, in the evening light.
And say that he should see the trains go by

in the spray of the sea, when the waves churn over the sleepers
Tell him – he ought to know the worst of me –
my head hurts and I called the little one
a filthy bitch for sicking up her milk
all over me. But now we're friends again.
Tell him that they carried the dog away

in his own pink blanket. I catch myself
stepping over where he used to lie
sprawling right across the kitchen. Tell him

he's not to worry – really, I'm doing fine.
On second thoughts, just tell him that I called

again, and I was sorry that I missed him.

Pigeons After Dark

With tennis-ball thuds,
clothes-brush sweeps,
pen-nib scratchings,

they punctuate
this ceaseless dirge
of sea and shingle,

mumbling small secrets
in the timbers, close above
my eggshell ceiling

as we wait,
almost together,
for the night
to finish.

Roisin's dream of escape

I cannot send you a starling – I must leave it to you
to look out of your window, and just *know* –
by the drift of smog, by foxes gibbering in the alleys,
by whatever speaks to you – that it is time.
Then you will go down to your Land Rover
and set out, guided by the morning star,
migrating gulls and motorway signs,
to where the railway borders the sea
on the dreary shores of the West.

By lunchtime you will be here – right here
in this house. Stooping to enter, standing
solid like a horse in the hallway. The Others
will not welcome you. There will be clattering,
clamour and consternation. Hands grabbing,
tugging at my clothes, to bundle me back
into the kitchen and lock the doors about me.

But you, in a gentle, brickwork-shaking murmur,
will explain that, today, everything has changed,
and send me upstairs to gather my things,
which will take no time. I have a Tesco's bag ready.
When I come down, it will be into the silence
of no more to be said. And you'll hoist me

up and over the broad ledge of your shoulder.
As we go, I'll raise my head just long enough to smile
through a tumbled curtain of hair, a smile of absolution –

for everything – upon a Pompeian tableau of Others
fixed in the slow-falling dust of the hallway.
Then out, rump first, into daylight.

Your boots will crunch over the gravel
and my fingers at your back will curl
in the rough green wool of your sweater.
The Hell train, grinding loud along the beach,
will salute us with a siren shriek of farewell,
as the damned lean from their carriage windows
to cheer us off. I shall wave an acknowledging foot.
The sun will glitter on all the shifting ridges of the sea –

but no more of *that*. Not another glance
at the empty horizon. Fold me, then, into that waiting car
and I will slide on warm leatherette. Lean above me,
pull the seatbelt over me, and already
I shall be breathing the slower breath of sleep.

Tinea trinotella

Out from the ceiling-cracks,
they whir on the moonscape walls, until
watch-spring trajectories deliver them

down to this corner I have made
so bright. Little scraps of gold-leaf,
furled and etched with hieroglyphs
too small to read, they wander
in scorching light, over the table,

over the pencilled image of a saint,
and over me, filling my frazzled hair
with the shiver of wings.

When We Come Out of the West

Bring me back to the City. Take my arm to steer me
among the bus stops, blasted pillar boxes and Jehovah's witnesses.
Find me colonnades to saunter through, fountains to drench me,
and buy balloons for this, my homecoming. Don't laugh
if you catch me photographing statues or tracing a finger
along the flaking curls of iron railings.
Come with me to buy shoes, so I can go without hurt
over the cobbles – except when I stumble. Which I will.
You'll grow used to this. Learn to catch me.
Loiter with me in the caverns of Euston;
describe the saris and the shtreimels, teetering headscarves
and gauzy rainbow trousers. The citizens will point
and make their children stare at us. Don't mind this –
hold my arm, tight, and keep me walking.

Move me into your rooms; I don't take up much space,
but I will strew paper everywhere. That's what I do.
Carry me to bed, sometimes. The long sighs of cars
out on the Westway, and a bewildered robin
singing to the streetlamps, might soothe me into sleep,
no longer troubled by dreams of the sea.
I'll bring you instant coffee in the mornings;
we'll stand at your window, timing the passage of clouds
between the chimneys.

In summer we'll dine with your expensive friends
and go drinking with the cheap ones. Light their faces

with bottled candles – I might even speak to them.
Dirty jokes – with all the different voices –
or stories of the waiting souls in hollow trees;
I can do it all. I'll make you proud of me.
But cut my food for me, without my asking,
if the lights go down too early.
On days of storms, when no one else is out
and the sky is darker than the rooftops,
I'll be up and gone before you've dressed,
searching in streets that have forgotten me
for where the printer's shop once stood,
or sheltering under the bandstand in the park,
mumbling the song of the monkey in the cellar.
But promise you'll be there when the rain won't come.
On your busiest days, release me in the museum
and let me roam in labyrinths of glass
where I will grow smaller
and younger through the drowsy afternoon.
Collect me at sunset, after closing. I'll be the last one,
sitting high up on the stone steps,
pretending to look out for you.

Black Swans at Sunrise

Between first light and the hour when dogs come out,
the black swans rise from the stream. They promenade
over the Lawns, and on the asphalt path,
curling their necks, selecting where to set

their feet, they go as slow as this
primordial mist about the rhododendrons.
The new sun spikes between the willow leaves

behind them, and I blink in a blur of tears.
The bench is coffin-cold; the seat of my jeans
is steeped in last night's rain. I hold
my sketchbook roofwise on my thigh,

and I am leaning back, and laughing,
because the marks that I have made
are not like swans, or anything.

The Art of Self-portraiture

If you send me a photograph – whether or not
your jawline is how I imagined – I'll fix you to my wall,
lie down beneath you, tell you secrets and undress
before your face at bedtime, with all the lamps still on.
And I would answer with a snapshot of my own.
But I've been careless – the children got in here
as I was sleeping, and now my father's camera lies
in irreconcilable pieces. So, I will draw my likeness

for you. Though it's your move, I shall make a start
while there is light descending in a blank sky,
over the water, and slamming into this room.
There are no warm flesh tones here – I'm only stark white
and shadows. I've made a place to lean the mirror,
and here are the broken ruler, the tape-measure
and rusty calipers, No, there is not much freehand here

anymore. I'm all geometry, and join-the-dots now. You see,
the losing of art is a slow thing, like the death of trees.
Perhaps you've noticed signs already, in my later pages –
an ill-proportioned salmon, or a wandering chicken
on some cobbled street whose head is just too big;
the lopsided grins of the beetle-chasers in the lane;
and how the bell-tower leaned far out of kilter
until all buildings turned to charcoal smudges, lost
in the sea-fog. To shape a single face, these days,
I must make such a scaffold of lines. Take my eyes –
so far apart, I have to plot their latitude

against the perpendicular. Of course, I press too hard –
no watercolour wash will hide these marks.
So, you will always see my face like this –
quartered by a cross. I wanted to smile at you
and show you every glistening, naked tooth. But this
will be a long labour. So, you can have my nothing face.
My somewhere-far-from-here face. To make amends
I'll tug the neckline of my T-shirt down, to bare
one shadowed clavicle, and the hollow of my throat. And then,

there is my hair. That will be fun. I do good hair,
even now. The wilder, the more frazzled, the more
backward-through-hedges, the better I scrawl it.
I will go crazy with this hair, and make so much of it –
because these days will end untidily. And soon,
with torn and scrunched-up paper lying everywhere. And no
final masterpiece amid the rubbish. These pencils, pens
and sable brushes won't be laid aside, packed in a drawer,
or handed down on some remembered day – only mislaid,
scattered, rattling down the stairs, rolling
into cracks and dark corners.

If We Should Ever Meet

and take a shine to each other — and if
we really did decide to be "in love" — well,
how would that go? I see the start of it;
we'd have our way of stepping out, hand in hand,
with me announcing dogshit, kerbs and things,
and I'd be banging every wheelie bin like it was
a bass drum,
clearing clutter off the pavement. Waiters would wait
for you,

and shop assistants bloody would assist – I'd see to that.
And happen everyone we knew would smile to see us
come hobbling through the crowd at this one's launch
or that one's private view. Because to them you'd be
an *inspiration* – like those crippled athletes on the telly.
I'd be so proud to take you everywhere. Mind you –
sometimes
it might be easier to park you, just for a minute,
outside the offy or the paper shop. And come October
when the clocks go back, then we'd agree you might be
better off

stopping indoors; but still, the rest of us
would raise a bottle to an absent friend – and somebody
would say that you reminded them of how exquisite
broken statues are. (Some of them really talk like that.)
And we'd imagine you, at home, sat still,
in a sort of holy rapture, with slow jazz playing
just above a whisper on your little radio. Except –

it wouldn't be like that, would it? You'd bang
against the walls, like some trapped bird; or try
to paint again, with twenty lamps plugged in at once,
and burn the fucking place down; or you'd go
to buy cheap wine from Sainsbury's, then get lost
down in the backstreets, twist your ankle
and end up lying in some gutter.

Even in the house, you'd catch yourself
on handlebars and wheels, whenever you forgot
my bike
was leaning in the hall – and knowing you,
you'd *always* be forgetting, with your head
still full of scary, beardy saints and magic snakes
and all that Celtic stuff. I see you crack your skull
on doors that I'd forget to close, and scald yourself
with every cup of tea I'd ever fetch you.
And how you'd bitch about it, like you do
in all these letters. I'd apologize, of course; and then
keep on – and on – apologizing. I would buy you

Braille machines and all the gear you needed,
when the time came; I see you in the attic,
typing God knows what, and only coming down to eat
when I've gone out. And I see me, forever working late
or taking evening classes in Chinese,
or having it away with some new temp – or anything

to keep out of the way. This morning, half awake
between the sunrise and my first alarm, I saw the kids
we might have had – a row of pale, mardy little freaks

who'd never run outside, or kick a ball about,
or climb a tree. When I woke up, here was
your latest letter, still unopened, lying there
on the locker, beside the framed cartoon
of how you said you thought of me.

Mice Will Sing on the Sea

Consider *this* for a synopsis, then:
We see a child; there is so much that he
might do. Instead, he grows up to be you;
you get a job in publishing, you marry
your secretary, get divorced, et cetera.
And then… it's some December afternoon.
A chill might softly fall about your shoulders
just as you go beyond the realm of sunlight
and central heating, down into the basement
under your mock Georgian Sussex farmhouse
where you keep the Christmas decorations

(along with legal documents, old clothes,
Swiss porn, and silver cups for playing squash).
It shouldn't take a minute – after this,
there will be coffee, calls to make, and rugby
on television. Halfway down the steps
you'll miss your footing, and just for a moment
you'll understand what real life is like.

Rain will fall on your garden. And sometimes
your telephones will ring in empty rooms –
though not so often, as the weeks go by.
And then, in time, the mice will come inside.
Diffidently, just a few at first.
But when they find it safe, they will come swarming,

and soon they'll gnaw and scratch in every room.

Of course, the warrior mice, the orator mice,
and other mice destined to leave their mark
will take the kitchen, staking out new fiefdoms
across your marble-look Formica worktops
and in your cupboards, where they will carouse
and feast on your organic wholemeal bread.
But limping, hobbling, tumbling down the steps
into the basement will come the outcast mice;
the crippled, stunted and asthmatic mice.

And this will be their haven (once they've crossed
the mountain that is you.) They'll live inside
the classical guitar you never played,
and every mouse-breath, every whisker-twitch
will set the strings vibrating. Thus they'll learn
to harmonize; and they shall make up songs
of you, their benefactor. They will cluster
around you in the dark, and sing to you.

And winter rains will overfill the rivers,
pushing your front doors and French windows in,
and all your Queen Anne furniture will go
with trees, with cars and cattle, to the sea.
Cold water will be rising in the basement,
but this is not the end. Now, your guitar
will be a ship – though bumped by your possessions
in plastic bags that roll like dying whales,
yet it will float, and all its crew will sing
The Last Farewell, as they go with the current,
over the gardens and the roads. And you –
you'll probably be food for eels, and crabs.

Some evenings, when their vessel is becalmed,
the mice will gather on the sunburst deck
and sing of you again. This will be rare,
however, for by now they'll be forgetting
the words, and why they mattered. Anyway,

there will be so much else to sing about.
They'll sing of the horizon; of the clouds;
the dread of seagulls. And by day they'll crouch
below decks as they listen to the wind
above them in the strings, and they'll rehearse
new anthems for an undiscovered land.

Monster Child (Roisin Leaves a Note)

Today will be hard. You will lurk in dusty half-light,
hands and feet braced high in the kitchen door-frame,
until your limbs are aching, the gappy grin begins
drooping at the corners, and no one comes downstairs
to be terrified.

I had meant to go by degrees, huddling
into smaller corners, taking on the colour of the walls,
whispering in time with the breaking waves
until no one could quite say whether I was here

or not. But fading takes so long.
Autumn has begun already, and my window
has never had curtains. I've been measuring
the falling length of days, and soon
the roads will freeze. I will try
to close the door softly behind me.

Today, you will have to stomp loudly on the stairs,
little monster, and yell for your breakfast.
Louder than your mother's swearing nightmares.
So loud that you will scare away the pigeons.
Soon, you will *all* go stomping through these rooms,
roaring my name in chorus. Remember that.

I have left you the book of how to draw skeletons
and breasts, and all the paints and pastels I don't need.
Television will light your face; your mother will sing;

your father will come, sometimes, out of the trees,
and now and then the cat will walk his slow requiem
down the span of the piano keys, in memory
of the dog – now beatified. And you, my monster –
you will learn to go loping over the Exeter Road
with no one beside you, clutching at your hand.
Your teetering cities of *Lego* and card will rise
and sprawl in my room where, maybe,
you will name a street after me.

These Notes Were for a Sequel, Never Finished

I
The library's dust floats in the windows' light.
An old man's footsteps are afternoon-quiet
among the rolling stacks. He carries a book
as though it were sleeping in his arms.

II
With tweezers, set the blue husk of a fly
beneath the lens. Copy, in shaky pencil,
the veins of its membrane wings. Remember
these bordered cells – the shapes in the chapel windows.

III
Grannie sang loud in the dark, like
a fractured fiddle – *on us, thy poor children,*
bestow a sweet smile… Saint Patrick, in plastic,
glowed green among crumpled tissues, packets
of pills, dentures smiling in their underwater sleep.

IV
A novice nun is scribing in her cell, breathing
her new-learned Latin words. After the quill
is laid down, all the white lights of her migraine flash across
the furrowed sea that fills the breadth of her window.

V

… no lacework of a cast-off skin, no hollow tooth,
or bone, or sigmoid trail in ancient rocks was ever found
to show that snakes might once have lived
anywhere on the island of Ireland…

VI
Children are running, swearing,
in and out of the fountain spray
outside, in the library gardens,
leaping to headbutt the sunflowers,
throwing their caps at dragonflies.

A Room in the City

My hands know every nubble of the wallpaper.
The wind still shuffles about behind the fireplace.
On better days, I go downstairs for dinner;
tomorrow we shall have paper hats – it's Christmas
on television. We carried up the angled lamp
to stand it by my bed, bending above the pillow.
The rooftops opposite, the aerials, the stunted trees
like broccoli, forming my skyline are the same

but farther off. The birds that come and go
are more like shadow puppets now,
and never call my name across the street.
I may look out at half past three,
my head upon the windowsill, to watch
a tangerine and silver sunset.
Or I may not.

So many of the books I learned to read
in my cocoon of eiderdown and blankets
are here, lined up and leaning on the shelves. Today,
I took one down and opened it, and every page
was white. I think of all the letters I have known
dancing their spider-conga down in the narrow space
behind the cupboards. The phone rings in two rooms,
and I am not afraid; I know it won't be anyone for me.

I close this book. I lie here, until teatime,
stare up at the light-bulb, watch the plankton
drifting in the fishbowl of my eye, and half my head
is in and out of dreams; a man stands on the iron bridge
and shouts, and points to stars that are not there. How small
he looks from here. The clowns are crawling on the roof

and laughing in the chimney. Pigeons flap in empty rooms,
the starfish hands of children wave through clouds reflected
in the windows of a long white car, and on a beach, a woman
rolls in the surf, an arm flops from a floral-patterned sling,
and snow is falling on the tracks, and on the sea,
covering all the broken wooden boats
in silence. And someone on the wall calls out
to ask me what I know. But I am gone, already.

The central heating clanks all through the house.
The tumble drier is growling, down in the kitchen,
and in the next room, someone moves about, and sings along,
off-key, with *The Seekers' Greatest Hits*.
I am a child, sitting up in bed, pressing
my ear to the wall.

Notes

p.1 *bananas of migrainous light...* Since childhood I have often been aware of flashing lights, usually elongated and curved, at the edges of my vision. Whether these are peculiar to my (and Roisin's) condition or are a more typical feature of migraine, I have been unable to determine. As a child, to my parents' utter bafflement, I would attempt to alert them to the phenomenon by announcing an attack of the *flashing white bananas*. As an adult I would be more likely to describe them as elliptical flashes, but my younger self's interpretation seemed apt for a poem about things barely recalled from childhood.

p.3 *a Mona Lisa with a spliff...* Novelty prints of the Mona Lisa, amended to depict her with one hand raised and holding an enormous spliff, were popular in the 1990s, and probably still are, among people of a particular mindset, intent on maintaining the illusion that, irrespective of the advancing years, they remain cool so long as they keep on smoking the weed (or "dope", as it then was). There are a *lot* of these people in South Devon. An image search on the internet will reveal several variations of the picture.

p.6 *a Vargas girl pose...* Alberto Vargas (1896-1982) was a Peruvian artist whose paintings of provocatively posed nude and partially-nude women are considered among the finest examples of "pin-up" art. His famous "Vargas girls" (published under the variant "Varga girls" during his tenure with *Esquire* magazine) were popular with Allied troops during World War II and even adorned the nose-cones of US bomber planes.

p.6 *his Barleybright*. The novelist Henry Williamson used the name "Barleybright" to denote his idealized perfect female companion. The prototype is a fictional character in his part-novel-part- autobiography *The Sun in the Sands*, generally acknowledged as being based on the young Anne Courtenay Edmonds (later Anne Welch, OBE,) with whom he was besotted but who did not return his affections – because, as he saw it, she had no interest in anything other than aeroplanes. (He may have had a point; Anne went on to become a renowned aviator, writing many books on the subject, and worked for the Air Transport Service during World War II, flying Spitfires and other planes from the factories where they were built to the airfields whence they were deployed. She eventually married Lorne Welch, a fellow pilot and former prisoner of war, who had designed the air pumps used in the tunnels for the "Great Escape" from Stalag Luft, and who, after being transferred to Colditz, worked on the legendary but never-completed escape plan involving a secretly constructed glider. Exactly the kind of bloke who ends up getting the girl.) The name "Barleybright" was subsequently applied by Williamson, in his journals and letters, to a succession of women – generally rather younger than Williamson himself – with whom he became temporarily infatuated.

p.6 *those bark-and-leather hands...* The reference is, perhaps inevitably, to Ted Hughes' poem 'Hands' (from his 1979 collection, *Moortown Diary*);

> You used them with as little regard
> As old iron tools – as if their creased, glossed crocodile leather Were nerveless...

p.6 *Larsen traps...* The Larsen cage trap is used by gamekeepers to trap magpies and other corvids. It consists of two cage compartments, one containing a live captive magpie as "bait". The local territorial bird, approaching to investigate or challenge the perceived intruder, is trapped in the other compartment. Sometimes a painted wooden model is used instead of a live decoy. The Larsen trap is still used in Britain but is outlawed in some countries, including Denmark where it was invented, being considered inhumane.

p.7... *the Adze-head*... This was a name, or nickname, applied to Saint Patrick. It seems to have been coined by his enemies, the Druids whose belief system and way of life he strove to eradicate in the course of his missionary work. An early biographer, Murchiu, records the supposed Druidic prophecy:

> Across the sea will come Adze-head, crazed in the head, his cloak with hole for the head, his stick bent in the head.
> He will chant impieties from a table in the front of his house; all his people will answer, *so be it, so be it*.

One theory is that the name refers to his tonsured haircut, which may have looked to the indigenous people as though the top of his head had been lopped off with an adze. I think it may have something to do with the mitre he is usually depicted as wearing, which looks somewhat like an axe blade. Whatever its origin, the name was taken up and used by the very pro-Patrick author of the *Acallam na Senórach* (*Tales of the Elders of Ireland* or *Colloquy of the Ancients*), who may have chosen to interpret it as expressing the Saint's strength and ruthlessness – the text places far more emphasis on these qualities than on gentleness or mercy.

p.7...*fistfuls of young clover*... The "shamrock" is of course a widely recognized symbol of Saint Patrick and of Ireland itself, due to the legend of how the Saint is supposed to have used the three-leaves at the top of its stem to illustrate the Mystery of the Holy Trinity – the Christian tradition of a single God who yet exists as the three persons of the Father, Son and Holy Spirit. (In fact, the first recorded accounts of this story appeared centuries after Saint Patrick's death). At the

Catholic school I attended, and elsewhere, the notion was fostered that "shamrock" was a rare and special plant, more or less endemic to Ireland, whence it was even exported so that Irish expat communities could keep the tradition of wearing a stem or sprig affixed to the clothing on Saint Patrick's Day (the 17th March). But it seems we were misled – in fact, a "shamrock" is simply a young sprig of any of various common and widespread species of clover, of the genus *Trifolium*.

p.7 *the drinking song his giant henchmen sing...* In the *Acallam na Senórach*, Saint Patrick encounters a wandering band of giant warriors from Ireland's pagan past, led by Cailte, once second-in-command to the legendary hero Finn mac Cumaill, who have somehow survived for over two centuries. Patrick befriends and baptises them, and they travel with him, sometimes acting as his enforcers and occasionally digging up treasures from the graves of their dead contemporaries to boost the coffers of Patrick's church. Though we are told that great age has impaired his memory, Cailte can recall enough from the pagan past to regale Patrick interminably with stories from his own time, which Patrick instructs his scribes to write down.

Whenever their journeying brings them to places that hold a special significance for him, Cailte breaks into song or poetry. One lengthy song recounts the names and capacities of the legendary drinking horns in the house of the *Fian*;

> Drink for eighty from Mudán,
> drink for a hundred from pure Grugán;
> Fair-Youthful the horn that Oscar brought to the
> assembly – it was the cynosure of foreign hosts,
> and women smiled to see
> it... et cetera and so forth.

p.7... *scrubbed and mouth-soaped...* In primary school, we had at least one teacher who would routinely threaten us with the traditional punishment of having our mouths washed out with soap and water for swearing. ("And not nice soap, either! I'll use carbolic soap and it will make you *sick!*") In this imagined scenario, the children are being made presentable for their new lives as little Christians, and any mouth-soapings are likely to have been administered not for profanity but for lapses into the words and rituals of the indigenous Celtic religion.

p.7... *a prayer for solid ground*... The specific reference is to the fate of the unfortunate Becán (see next note), but there is also a more general reference to an ongoing Celtic preoccupation. The Celts portrayed themselves in their oral and written traditions as a proud warrior race, equal to any mortal foe, claiming to fear no other thing than that the very elements of the world itself should betray them. In *Myths and Legends of the Celtic People*, T.W. Rolleston draws attention to the striking parallel between Ptolemy Soter's account of the Ionian Celts' pledge of alliance with Alexander the Great – "If we observe not this engagement, may the sky fall and crush us, may the earth gape and swallow us up, may the sea burst out and overwhelm us"– and a passage from the Irish epic, the *Táin bo Cuailgne*, written over a thousand years later; "Unless the sky shall fall with its showers of stars on the ground where we are camped, or unless the earth shall be rent by an earthquake, or unless the waves of the blue sea come over the forests of the living world, we shall never give ground." The imagery of the potentially treacherous earth would strike a particular chord with Roisin; one of the symptoms of Retinitis Pigmentosa is the loss of night-vision. When travelling in dim light, the constant fear is that the next footstep might land on something unpleasant – or worse, on nothing.

p.7... *the sinner's cattle*... One story in the *Acallam na Senórach* tells of Saint Patrick, his retinue of scribes and his new friends, the partially senile giant warriors of the *Fian*, arriving at the house of Becán and asking for food and lodging for the night. Becán declines the request. A lesser man might content himself with a simple "Well, fuck you, then," before going on his way, but the Saint does not let it lie. He voices his wish that "none of Becán's people or cattle be alive tomorrow," and immediately the ground opens and swallows Becán and his entire household, along with all his livestock. Patrick takes it upon himself to give Becán's lands and titles to his more obliging brother, Fulartach.

p.8 *a new grey mantle…* The long-deceased crow whose bones Roisin still has in her keeping, would have been a carrion crow (*Corvus corone*), the familiar all-black crow of most of the British Isles. For his afterlife as a character in an illustrated children's book, however, he is destined to undergo a change of species. Because the story is to be set in Ireland, he will be re-imagined as a hooded crow (*Corvus cornix*), the species that replaces the carrion crow in Ireland and parts of northern Scotland. The hooded crow is black on the head, throat and upper breast, wings, tail and legs, with the rest of the plumage a beautiful soft grey. Coloration aside, the two forms are practically identical, and were, until just a few years ago, considered to be geographical variants of a single species.

p.8 *the lullabies he sometimes sings…* Birds of the crow family are true songbirds, even if they are not always thought of as such. They use song not to proclaim territorial rights, as other songbirds do (the simple, resonant "caw" suffices for that purpose) but seemingly for their own amusement. In what is known as a "sub-song", a solitary crow will sometimes entertain itself with a bizarre and endearing monologue of chirps, croaks, gurgles, clicks and squeaks.

p.9 *kingfishers, hares and hawks…* Without naming names, it appears that hares (even those whom hound did ne'er pursue) and hawks (in or out of the rain) are part of the established stock-in-trade of the "nature poet" – understandably so, given that they are such striking and evocative animals. Kingfishers are a great favourite with visual artists and this was especially apparent throughout my sojourn in the West Country. The arts and crafts shops of Exeter and Torquay were perennially filled with watercolours by local artists of varying degrees of ability, depicting kingfishers. The bird was invariably portrayed poised on a post or twig as though about to launch itself at an unsuspecting fish below. (Paintings depicting kingfishers attempting to drown one another in territorial disputes or devouring their neighbours' chicks would have offered a broader insight into the biology of the species and a greater variety of composition, but I never saw any such pictures.) Yet for a visually impaired person who cannot easily travel alone in wild places, such creatures are the stuff of fable, far removed from one's own experience. The bluebottle that you peer at through a hand-lens after nearly failing to notice it floating drowned in your coffee is *real*, and experienced at first hand, and is so much more redolent of the natural world in all its wonder.

p.9 *I claim the heron for a totem...* Herons are another species often associated with wild, remote locations – not least, the *heron priested shore* of Dylan Thomas' 'Poem in October'. Fortunately for those who cannot get to such places, however, they appear not to realize that their imposing stature and fiercely primal appearance demand an appropriately dramatic setting, and are just as happy stalking fish from the banks of ponds in London parks and gardens. A few years ago, I was regularly woken by a chorus of pissed-off crows and magpies to the sight of a heron looking utterly incongruous on the rooftop across the street from my bedroom window – presumably eyeing up the fishpond in the garden of that house whilst ignoring the mobbing crows with unshakeable gravitas. (I've never seen crows bothering a heron on the ground or at the water's edge, but they immediately take exception if the same heron flies up into a tree or onto a roof. Crows seem to have a clearly defined sense of where herons belong, and where they don't.)

p.9 *a babble of unseen finches...* I'm thinking especially of goldfinches here. And greenfinches. I seem to hear them *everywhere* in the summer months, but I have never caught even the most fleeting glimpse of either species. Not once.

p.10 *Death's head moths... like the ghosts of mice.* The death's head hawk moth (*Acherontia atropos*) is an unusually noisy species of moth, capable of emitting shrill squeaks by expelling air through its proboscis. Its main sustenance is honey stolen from beehives, and the sound is believed to be a means of deterring any defensive action on the part of the bees whilst the moth is on the rob. To my ear, the sound is like the squeaking of mice but with a more reedy, slightly spooky quality.

p.11 *the gulls that moan like babies on the roof...* The best-known call of the herring gull (*Larus argentatus*) is the classic "seagull" sound, but it has a broad vocabulary of other calls. Whilst living and child- minding in Torquay and Dawlish, I learned that those uttered when perched on a roof include a variety of moans and wails that sound precisely like a small child with its arm stuck under the fridge. It was with uncanny frequency that, immediately after running into the next room to deal with a child-centred emergency – whilst simultaneously thinking up a feasible excuse for the neglect that allowed said emergency to arise – and after finding that the alarm was false, with all children safely accounted for, I would hear that other gull-call that sounds like a low, sniggering laugh.

p.11 *an hour away...* Other than the "half-remembered books" from even farther back, Roisin's oldest clear memories of childhood reading are of Henry Williamson's *Salar the Salmon* – an even lovelier book than his better-known *Tarka the Otter*. As with most of Williamson's nature stories, the setting is among the waterways of north Devon, particularly the River Bray, near Barnstaple. Hence, much of Roisin's most cherished mental hinterland concerns places and creatures she has never seen, in a dreamed-of world that was once remote but, now that she is in Devon – without help or access to transport – is very close, whilst remaining entirely beyond her reach. (According to Google, the distance from Dawlish to the River Bray is 59 miles, with an estimated travel time of one hour and ten minutes.)

p.12 *oolypuggers... pollywiggles... ream...* In a letter to the *London Mercury* in 1928, Henry Williamson provided a glossary of unfamiliar terms used in *Tarka the Otter* and elsewhere in his work – a few were of his own invention, but most belonged to the rural West Country dialect. *Oolypuggers* are waterside reeds; "the great mace reed, commonly called a bull-rush... the white mores (roots) making a puggy noise in ooze when pulled... Was not language first made in the child-mind of man?" A *pollywiggle* is a tadpole. A *ream* is the "arrowy ripple" or wave created by a fish when its dorsal fin breaks the water surface.

p.12 *the mending of the kelt...* a kelt is a salmon that has recently spawned. Most die of exhaustion, starvation and disease, but a few make it back to the sea where, in the vernacular of West Country fishermen, they "mend" or "clean" themselves. In a passage in *Salar the Salmon*, Williamson describes how, poignantly, this "mending" process begins *before* the return to the sea, with the nearly-spent fish's last reserves used in preparation for the better times that just might be ahead, growing new teeth and a silvery brine-proof outer layer on the skin and scales, imparting a lustrous and as-yet misleading appearance of restored health;

> ... thus is the kelt, exhausted salmon, reborn – its bright scales and sharp teeth a death-desperate hope of resurrection.

p.13 *the convex washer-ring of his eye...* It seems to me that the eye of a fish resembles a "Belleville" washer, which differs from the standard flat washers (metal discs with a hole in the centre) used for load-bearing and spacing in most household taps and other plumbing systems) in having a slightly conical shape. (According to a Wikipedia article, this "provides an axial force when deformed". Whatever that means.)

p.14 *the seagulls snigger from the rooftops...* See earlier note on gulls.

p.14 *the Red Arrows...* The spectacular displays of the Royal Air Force Aerobatic Team, informally called the Red Arrows, were such a familiar sight over Dawlish when I lived there that I became – mistakenly – convinced they were based nearby. In fact their base at that time was at RAF Cranwell in Lincolnshire. Even allowing that my memory must have exaggerated the frequency of their appearances, how they were able to maintain such a regular presence remains baffling.

p.17 *I cannot send you a starling...* In the Second Branch of the *Mabinogion*, Branwen, the sister of the giant Welsh king Bran, is married to Matholwch, the king of Ireland. Angered by the insulting behaviour of Bran's and Branwen's younger brother, the troublemaker Evnissyen, Matholwch rejects his new bride shortly after returning with her to Ireland, and sets her to work as a slave in his kitchens, where she is subjected to regular beatings by the cook. Fearing reprisals should the Welsh find out what he has done, Matholwch imposes a ban on all sea traffic between Ireland and Britain. With no other means of sending a message, Branwen trains a pet starling which carries a letter to Bran's court in Wales. The resulting war annihilates almost the entire populations of both Britain and Ireland. Though Branwen is among the few survivors, she dies of grief soon after her return to Wales.

p.19 *Tinea trinotella* – the "Bird's Nest Moth". This species is a member of the "clothes moth" family, but unlike some of its relatives, is seldom a pest of woollen fabrics, and usually breeds in old bird nests, especially those of chickens and pigeons, where the larvae feed on old feathers and other detritus. The pigeon-haunted attic above Roisin's bedroom would be an ideal habitat. Some other clothes moth species are supposedly not drawn to light, but the Bird's Nest Moth, as I can personally vouch, is strongly attracted to desk lamps and, presumably, other light sources.

p.19 *my frazzled hair...* Literally. In the '90s, before the advent of energy saving lightbulbs, singed hair as a result of working too close to a desk lamp with a traditional incandescent bulb was a perennial hazard for the visually impaired artist.

p.20... *the saris and the shtriemels...* A sari is, of course, a long, flowing garment – often made of several beautifully coloured fabrics – traditionally worn by women in India, Pakistan, Sri Lanka and other South Asian countries. A shtriemel is a hat, often with a rim or covering of fur, worn by men among Hasidic Jews (and some other Orthodox Jewish communities). I have a distinct memory of arriving at one of the big London stations after a long sojourn in Dawlish (which, in the 1990s, had not yet heard of multiculturalism), and being entranced by these and a great many other traditional national costumes among the crowds.

p.20... *the citizens will point...* Diversity, however, does have its limits. Even in the Metropolis there is one way to stand out in a crowd. The disabled have no country.

p.21 *the song of the monkey in the cellar.* Some time in the early 1980s, the 'Peckham Rocks' festival took place at the bandstand in Peckham Rye Park (which is no longer there). One of the headline acts was "Rocko, the Peckham Poet" who, accompanying himself on an acoustic guitar, entertained the crowd (such as it was) with an ingeniously worked out set of songs themed around the monkey- like cave-dwellers that he imagined inhabiting Ancient Peckham a million years before the first human settlement. The ballad 'If I Only Had Time' – though generally attributed to the French singer Michel Fugain, (made famous in its English-language version by John Rowles) – was in fact, said Rocko, first sung in Peckham's primal forests by the young males of the species as they reflected on the prospect of brief, brutal lives that were certain to end violently in inter-tribal conflict. The lyrics to other songs were supposed to have been translated from primitive writings found on the rock walls of a cave that had subsequently become a pub cellar. Unfortunately, Rocko appears to have left no mark on cultural history whatsoever, and I can find no record of the festival either. (I know it happened; my sister and I were there.) Therefore this is a reference that absolutely nobody will ever "get". However, I left it in because it felt right.

p.22 *black swans...* The Australian black swan (*Cygnus atratus*) is often found among collections of exotic waterfowl, and appears to be establishing itself in the wild at various locations across the British Isles, but holds a special, iconic significance for the town of Dawlish, where a small breeding population has existed for over forty years.

p.22 *the Lawns...* This is the name of a narrow park that effectively splits Dawlish's main high street down the middle. Aside from the beach, it is the town's main focal point for tourist activity, hosting fetes, fun fairs and, on the bandstand, various musical performances. The black swans that have become a Dawlish trademark live, with other waterfowl, on and around a stream that runs through the centre of the Lawns.

p.23 *the beetle-chasers in the lane.* Again, an obscure reference that simply felt right in poetic terms. In his 1903 memoir, *Hampshire Days*, the naturalist WH Hudson describes the flight of the stag beetle and the predictable response it provoked in the local children:

> When the beetle's flight takes him by village or hamlet, the children playing in the road... are suddenly thrown into a state of wild excitement, and starting to their feet, they run whooping after the wanderer, throwing their caps to bring him down.

p.25 *If We Should Ever Meet...* Brian speaks. Or does he?

p.25 *in a sort of holy rapture, with slow jazz playing...* The reference is to 'A System', by the late American poet Lynda Hull, which describes a meeting with a blind friend, with whom the speaker seems unable to empathize. Driving home afterward, she imagines what the friend might now be doing (apparently not much):

> ... I want her
> then, to sit quietly in a pure matrix
> of imagined light, darkness pressing down
> like rain as the radio plays stations
> from Baton Rouge, New Orleans and beyond.

p.29 *...the crippled, stunted and asthmatic mice... and they shall make up songs...* In the early 1950s, the Tasmanian mammologist Peter Crowcroft was employed by Britain's Ministry of Agriculture and Fisheries to research the behaviour and biology of mice, for the purposes of more effective control of mouse infestations in the large grain stores (buffer depots) that were maintained in case of import blockades during the Cold War era. To facilitate his research, he created an observable habitat for his subjects – his "Mouse House" – at a disused RAF base near Bury St Edmunds. His experiences were recounted in his book *Mice All Over*, which has become a classic of popular zoology. Previously, wild house mice had been little studied, and it had been assumed that mouse colonies were harmonious extended families. It turned out that they are fiercely hierarchical and territorial. Males that are not strong enough to defend territories are doomed to wander, becoming "hobo mice", trying to keep out of the way of the dominant individuals who persecute them relentlessly, and they probably do not survive for long under natural conditions. "They became so cowed that they no longer displayed aggression toward one another, but huddled together for warmth, and perhaps for comfort." Crowcroft used the term "singing mouse" for a mouse with a peculiar respiratory condition that caused it to emit a vocal squeak with every exhaled breath.

p.29 *The Last Farewell*... A song by the Kenyan singer Roger Whittaker, which first appeared on his 1971 album, *New World in the Morning*. While hosting a British radio show, Whittaker invited listeners to send in their lyrics so that he could select his favourites and set them to music. The lyric to 'The Last Farewell' was a poem by Ron Webster, a silversmith from Birmingham. The song was later covered by Elvis Presley (though the recording was not released until seven years after the King's death).

p.32 *cities of Lego*... Lego is a perennially popular children's toy, consisting of interlocking plastic blocks from which larger structures can be assembled. This probably requires no explanation, but I am mindful of an occasion when I was about eight and in hospital awaiting an operation, when a Lego brick thrown by the child in the adjacent bed broke a lens of my spectacles, giving me an eyeful of shattered glass. I distinctly recall that the junior doctor in the casualty department had no idea what Lego was and a nurse had to explain and spell it for him, for the purposes of the paperwork. This is true.

p.33 ...*on us, thy poor children*... From the hymn, 'Hail, Glorious Saint Patrick'. with a lyric by one Sister Agnes, set to a traditional Irish melody.

p.34 ...*no lacework of a cast-off skin*... This stanza is a "pretend quote" from an imaginary tome, but is substantially true. The legend of Saint Patrick's expulsion of Ireland's entire population of snakes appears to have been a symbolic representation of his eradication of the Druidic religion, which may have serpent imagery (it has been suggested that some Druids may even have adorned their skin with snake tattoos). As for actual snakes, there is no fossil evidence that they ever existed in Ireland in the first place. After the last Ice Age, sea levels were lower and both Britain and Ireland were part of mainland Europe, which enabled animals and plants to recolonize these regions. Approximately eight thousand five hundred years ago, Ireland was cut off from the continent by the formation of the Irish Sea, but the English Channel did not form until the sea level rose further, about two thousand years later. Various flora and fauna that are found in Britain but not in Ireland – including our three species of snakes – are believed to have arrived in Britain during this intervening period.